A BAD CASE
OF THE
GiGGLES

A BAD CASE OF THE GIGGLES

Kids Pick the Funniest Poems, Book #2

ILLUSTRATED BY
STEPHEN CARPENTER

EDITED BY
BRUCE LANSKY

Meadowbrook Press

Distributed by Simon & Schuster
New York

Library of Congress Cataloging-in-Publication Data

The Library of Congress has cataloged the hardcover edition as follows:

A Bad case of the giggles : kids' favorite funny poems / selected by
    Bruce Lansky ; illustrated by Stephen Carpenter.
            p. cm.
        Includes index.
        Summary: A collection of humorous poems by such authors as Jack
Prelutsky, Shel Silverstein, and other lesser-known poets.
        1. Humorous poetry, American. 2. Children's poetry, American.
    [1. American poetry—Collections. 2. Humorous poetry.] I. Lansky,
    Bruce. II. Carpenter, Stephen, ill.
PS595.H8B33 1994
811'.08089282—dc20   94-3336
                                                         CIP
                                                          AC

Paperback   ISBN 13: 978-0-88166-534-5 (Meadowbrook)
             ISBN 10: 1-4169-5197-0 (Simon & Schuster)
             ISBN 13: 978-1-4169-5197-1 (Simon & Schuster)

Editor: Bruce Lansky
Managing Editor: Dale E. Howard
Editorial Coordinator: Cathy Broberg
Art Director: Erik Broberg
Illustrator: Stephen Carpenter
Production Manager: Amy Unger
Desktop Coordinator: Patrick Gross

Published by Meadowbrook Press, 5451 Smetana Drive, Minnetonka, MN 55343

BOOK TRADE DISTRIBUTION by Simon & Schuster, a division of Simon and Schuster, Inc.,
1230 Avenue of the Americas, New York, NY 10020

12 11   10 9 8 7 6 5

Printed in the United States of America

ACKNOWLEDGMENTS

We would like to thank the following teachers and their students for helping us select the poems for this book:

Gloria Ameter, Clear Springs Elementary; Sherry Anderson, Schman Elementary; Diane Belcourt, Buffalo Primary; Kitty Crosby, Patty Edgren, and Jackie Robie, Blake Highcroft; Lori Eckert, Fran Olson, and Judy Roe, St. Anthony Park Elementary; Diane Erickson and Lois Pederson, Tanglen Elementary; Mary Fenwick and Polly Pfiefer, Minnetonka Intermediate School; Robin Frober and Dawn Hansen, Kids & Company; Paige Frondell and Ray Knoss, Eisenhower Elementary; Jane Hesselin, Sunset Hill Elementary; Marsha Jacobson, Hopkins School District; Mrs. Kostreba, Kim Lee, Ms. Mattheisen, Ms. McLeod, Jeanne Nelson, and Mrs. Thelen, St. Mary's Catholic School; Elaine Kroemer, Peter Robart School; Carol Larson, Mississippi Elementary; Sara Lovelace and Margaret Spriggs, Groveland Elementary; Lisa Muller and Mary Jo Schommer, Holy Name of Jesus; Jacky Naslund, Johnsville Elementary; Tessie Oconer, Fulton School; Mary Jane Savino, Barton School; and Vicki Wiita, Cumberland School District.

Special thanks to the parents who reviewed the manuscript:

Jim Bohen, Sonja and Mark Brown, Chris Bruce, Beth and Kevin Dooley, Susan Gray, Cynthia Gill, Julie Hanning, Laura Irvin, Jo S. Kittinger, Sydnie Meltzer Kleinhenz, Bill Kron, Ann Lynch, Jane Korn Madoff, Hilary Magnuson, Lori Reed, Dawn Trappen, and Julie Zumwalt.

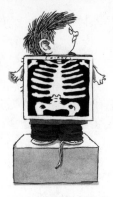

CONTENTS

Off to School We Go

What's for Dinner?

Critters

Tall Tales

INTRODUCTION

Hundreds of kids, parents, and teachers have told me that the anthology I published in 1991, *Kids Pick the Funniest Poems,* is the funniest book of poetry for school-age kids ever published. As flattered as I am to hear that comment, it makes me nervous as I write this introduction to a book that is essentially a sequel. How can this new book possibly be better than the best?

Well, I've done everything I could to make it better. I've searched for more funny poems from the most popular poets in the first book, including Shel Silverstein, Jack Prelutsky, Judith Viorst, Jeff Moss, John Ciardi, Bill Dodds, and Joyce Armor. I've also contacted scores of poets whose work did not appear in the first book and received some great new poems from Robert Scotellaro, Sylvia Andrews, Shirlee Curlee Bingham, Goldie Olszynko Gryn, and others.

And, I tested hundreds of poems on an expanded panel of school children and teachers to make sure that the very best poems would be selected for this book.

Is *A Bad Case of the Giggles* funnier than *Kids Pick the Funniest Poems?* You'll have to read them both to find out.

A Bad Case of the Giggles

I found a book of poems.
I brought the book to school.
And every time I look at it
I giggle like a fool.

Today in social studies
I opened up the book.
I started giggling right away
from just a single look.

I'm croaking like a bullfrog.
I'm braying like a mule.
These aren't sounds you're supposed to make
while studying at school.

The more I try to stop it,
the louder that I howl.
I'm squawking like a parrot,
and hooting like an owl.

I'm making a commotion;
the teacher is upset.
I'm losing my position here
as teacher's favorite pet!

My giggling is contagious;
my friends have all joined in.
The teacher's getting angry.
We're making quite a din.

The whole darned class is giggling.
Not one of us can stop.
The teacher says that if we can't
he'll call the hallway cop.

The room next door has heard us.
And now they're giggling too.
The sound of giggling travels fast.
The school sounds like a zoo.

And now the teacher's giving up.
He cannot teach today.
The principal's declaring it
a giggling holiday.

Bruce Lansky

I'm Thankful

I'm thankful for my baseball bat,
I cracked it yesterday,
I'm thankful for my checker set,
I haven't learned to play,
I'm thankful for my mittens,
one is missing in the snow,
I'm thankful for my hamsters,
they escaped a month ago.

I'm thankful for my basketball,
it's sprung another leak,
I'm thankful for my parakeet,
it bit me twice last week,
I'm thankful for my bicycle,
I crashed into a tree,
I'm thankful for my roller skates,
I fell and scraped my knee.

I'm thankful for my model plane,
it's short a dozen parts,
I'm thankful for my target game,
I'm sure I'll find the darts,
I'm thankful for my bathing suit,
it came off in the river,
I'm thankful for so many things,
except, of course, for LIVER!

Jack Prelutsky

Oh, Woe Ith Me!

Ath I wath biking
down the thtweet,
I hit a bump
and lotht my theat.

I cwathed my bike
into a twee,
I thcwathed my fathe,
oh, woe ith me.

My bike ith wecked,
I've no excuthe.
And wortht of all,
my tooth ith looth.

Bruce Lansky

3

I'm Going to Say I'm Sorry

I'm going to say I'm sorry.
It's time for this quarrel to end.
I know that we both didn't mean it
and each of us misses a friend.
It isn't much fun being angry
and arguing's just the worst,
so I'm going to say I'm sorry . . .
just as soon as you say it first!

Jeff Moss

4

I Have No Trouble Sharing

I have no trouble sharing—
I'm good at it, you'll find.
When I eat watermelon,
I always share the rind.

When there's a chore like cleaning
my filthy, dusty room—
I'm never, ever stingy.
I always share my broom.

And if you share your cookies
(I'm hoping that you do),
the next time I eat walnuts
I'll share the shells with you.

I think a kid like me is
so very, very rare.
A kid that has no trouble
with knowing how to share.

Robert Scotellaro

Soon

Soon I'll do the supper dishes,
sweep the carpet, feed the fishes,
clear the closet, take the dogs out,
do my homework, sort my rocks out,
clip my toenails, take a shower,
put away my two-foot tower,
file my records, clean my speakers,
shine my shoes and air my sneakers,
pick up socks and shirts and laces,
pack my cards in special cases,
dust my desk and all that's in it,
brush my teeth for one whole minute,
stack my comic-book collection,
call you in for room inspection.
But right now I'm really busy
and I'm starting to feel dizzy.
So I'll do what you requested,
just as soon as I'm well rested.

Goldie Olszynko Gryn

Smart

My dad gave me one dollar bill
'cause I'm his smartest son,
and I swapped it for two shiny quarters
'cause two is more than one!

And then I took the quarters
and traded them to Lou
for three dimes—I guess he don't know
that three is more than two!

Just then, along came old blind Bates
and just 'cause he can't see
he gave me four nickels for my three dimes,
and four is more than three!

And I took the nickels to Hiram Coombs
down at the seed-feed store,
and the fool gave me five pennies for them,
and five is more than four!

And then I went and showed my dad,
and he got red in the cheeks
and closed his eyes and shook his head—
too proud of me to speak!

Shel Silverstein

Stinky Feet

I free my feet from tennis shoes,
it feels so cool and fine.
But as I tread across the room,
I leave a scent behind.

I love it when I take them off,
the air feels so delish.
But then I hear my sister yell,
"Your feet smell like dead fish!"

"Put on your shoes, I'm gagging bad!"
My sister's such a fink.
Before she fakes a faint she cries,
"I'm passing out from stink!"

Shirlee Curlee Bingham

8

When Your Sucker Sticks

My sucker stuck to my sweater;
my sucker stuck in my hair.
Mum had to get the scissors
to cut it out of there.

All because of my sucker,
there's a bald spot on my head.
To tell the truth
I'd rather have
that sucker stuck instead.

Sheree Fitch

Insides

I'm very grateful to my skin
for keeping all my insides in—
I do so hate to think about
what I would look like inside-out.

Colin West

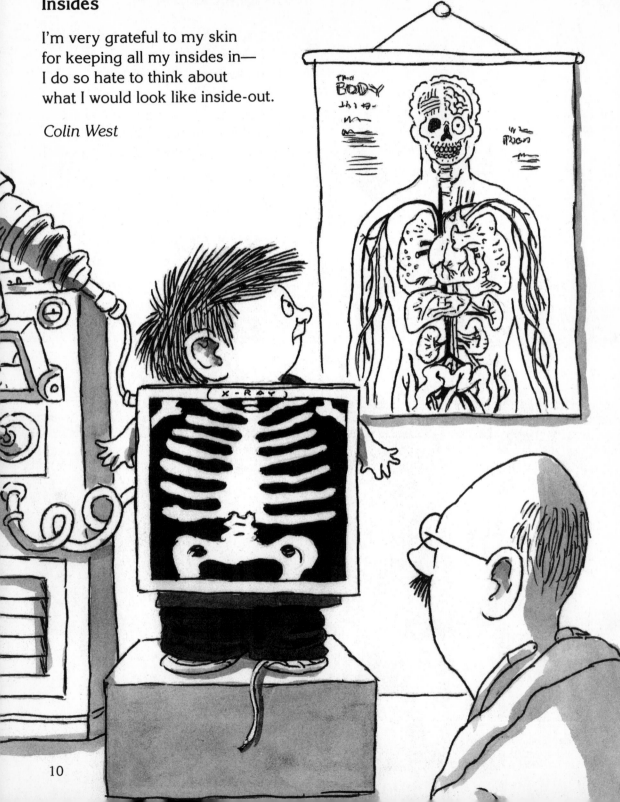

Funny Face

Suppose my nose were upside down:
In any rainstorm I might drown.
The sun would shine into my eyes
because my glasses sat so high.
One morning I'd hop out of bed
to find my mustache on my head.
And every time I'd sneeze or cough
the blast would blow my ballcap off.

Calvin Miller

Toes in My Nose

I bet that I could do it.
My friends all said, "No way."
And now my toes are in my nose,
so they will have to pay.

They each owe me a dollar.
Of that there is no doubt.
There's just one little problem.
I cannot get them out.

Bruce Lansky

How Dry I Am

How dry I am,
how wet I'll be,
if I don't find
the bathroom key.

There's not much time.
I cannot wait.
It would be awful
if I'm late.

I found the key.
It's on the floor.
Whoops! I don't need it
anymore.

Bruce Lansky

Backbite

Nothing makes me
quite retreat
like an ice-cold
toilet seat!

David Sudol

Pick Up Your Room

Pick up your room, my mother says
(she says it every day);
my room's too heavy to pick up
(that's what I always say).
Drink up your milk, she says to me,
don't bubble like a clown;
of course she knows I'll answer that
I'd rather drink it down.
And when she says at eight o'clock,
you must go right to bed,
we both repeat my answer:
why not go left instead?

Mary Ann Hoberman

16

Your Nose Is Running

"Your nose is running," Mother said.
I answered, "Wow! That's really neat!"
"Why's that?" she asked. I said, "Because
I never knew my nose had feet."

Jeff Moss

Millicent's Mother

Millie buttons her coat, gives her mother a kiss,
then Millicent's mother says something like this:
"Millie, take your umbrella in case there's a storm,
and be sure to wear mittens to keep your hands warm,
and, since it may snow, take your snowshoes and parka,
and pack your big flashlight in case it gets dark-a.
This bicycle pump will help fix a flat tire,
this fire extinguisher puts out a fire,
and take this roast turkey, you may need a snack,
this map and this compass will help you get back,
and take your galoshes, there may be some mud,
and your scuba-dive outfit in case there's a flood,
and in case you get bored, take your toys in your wagon,
and please wear your armor, in case there's a dragon."
"Oh, Mommy!" says Millie. "I don't need all that!"
"Okay," says her mother. "But wear a warm hat."

Jeff Moss

18

Mom's Diet

Whenever Mom goes on a diet,
she cooks weird food and makes me try it.

When she is hungry, she gets cranky.
If I'm not perfect, she might spank me.

She swims, she bikes, she runs, she dances.
I hope she'll soon fit in her pantses.

Bruce Lansky

I'm Telling!

Sam's the country's champion tattler,
boy is he a little rattler.
"Ashley's in the 'frigerator!"
"David's watching *Terminator!*"
"Kristin stayed up late last Monday!"
"Chad and Matt ditched church on Sunday!"
Now our boy's in quite a jam, for
EVERYBODY tells on Sam.

Joyce Armor

Living Doll

My Betsy Wetsy doll won't wet
and Bathtub Barbie drowned.
Drooling Dan has not drooled yet;
Burping Bob broke down.
Crying Chrissy doesn't cry
and Chatting Chet won't chat,
but that's okay because my baby
brother does all that!

Larry Cohen and Steve Zweig

My Noisy Brother

My brother's such a noisy kid,
when he eats soup he slurps.
When he drinks milk he gargles.
And after meals he burps.

He cracks his knuckles when he's bored.
He whistles when he walks.
He snaps his fingers when he sings,
and when he's mad he squawks.

At night my brother snores so loud
it sounds just like a riot.
Even when he sleeps
my noisy brother isn't quiet.

Bruce Lansky

23

A Baby Brother

I have a baby brother;
they brought him home last week.
He doesn't talk or play with me . . .
all he does is sleep.

Mom said that I could hold him.
I thought that might be fun;
but all he does is stare at me . . .
I think he's kind'a dumb.

Some say he looks like daddy.
Some say he looks like me.
I think they all need glasses . . .
he's bald as he can be.

If this is what a baby's like,
I think we'd be ahead
to try and get a refund . . .
and buy a dog instead.

Geraldine Nicholas

My Baby Brother

My baby brother is so small,
he hasn't even learned to crawl.
He's only been around a week,
and all he seems to do is bawl
and wiggle, sleep . . . and leak.

Jack Prelutsky

My Three Aunts

Aunt Patty pinches cheeks so hard
it leaves a dark red patch.
Aunt Mary makes me kiss her face,
which always has a rash.
Aunt Peggy pats my head so long
I feel like my dog Rover.
I hate it when my three aunts call
to say they're coming over.

Goldie Olszynko Gryn

Night Starvation or the Biter Bit

At night, my Uncle Rufus
(or so I've heard it said)
would put his teeth into a glass
of water by his bed.

At three o'clock one morning,
he woke up with a cough,
and as he reached out for his teeth—
they bit his hand right off.

Carey Blyton

Uncle Dave's Car

I pleaded with my Uncle Dave
to take us for a ride.
My sisters grabbed a window seat.
I sat right by his side.

He zoomed across a garden
and knocked some hedges down,
then barreled over sidewalks
in a busy part of town.

He zipped along a winding road—
a siren made him stop.
My uncle got a ticket from
a very angry cop.

At home our mother asked us,
"Did all of you behave?"
We answered her, "Of course we did."
(Except for Uncle Dave!)

Helen Ksypka

Grandma's Kisses

They're the biggest, wet, juiciest kisses in town.
When she gets you, you think that you're going to drown.
My brother and I always argue the worst
to make sure Grandma kisses the other one first.
Oh no, here she comes! Quick, let's dodge the explosion!
Too late! What a kiss! That's no kiss, that's an ocean!

Jeff Moss

Grandpa's Whiskers

Grandpa's whiskers long and gray,
always getting in the way.
Grandma chews them in her sleep,
thinking they are shredded wheat.

Anonymous

Christmas Thank You's

Dear Auntie
Oh, what a nice jumper
I've always adored powder blue
and fancy you thinking of
orange and pink
for the stripes
how clever of you

Dear Uncle
The soap is
terrific
so
useful and such a kind thought and
how did you guess that
I'd just used the last of
the soap that last Christmas brought

Dear Gran
Many thanks for the hankies
now I really can't wait for the flu
and the daisies embroidered
in red round the 'M'
for Michael
how
thoughtful of you

Dear Cousin
What socks!
and the same sort you wear
so you must be
the last word in style
and I'm certain you're right that the
luminous green
will make me stand out a mile

Dear Sister
I quite understand your concern
it's a risk sending jam in the post
but I think I've pulled out
all the big bits
of glass
so it won't taste too sharp
spread on toast

Dear Grandad
Don't fret
I'm delighted
so *don't* think your gift will
offend
I'm not at all hurt
that you gave up this year
and just sent me
a fiver
to spend

Mick Gowar

33

Hand-Me-Downs

I'm always wearing hand-me-downs.
I don't get stuff that's new.
My mom won't take me shopping.
I don't know what to do.
The dresses always fit me fine,
but high heels give me blisters.
It's not that easy growing up,
a boy with older sisters.

Bob Zanger

Today Is Not a Good Day

Today is not a good day.
I woke up sick in bed.
My stomach has a stabbing pain
that's spreading to my head.
My knees are weak and achy.
My eyes are full of flu.
I fear I may contaminate;
I have a fever too.
I cannot see.
I cannot breathe.
I cannot read or write.
My eyes are shut,
my nose is blocked,
I'm not a pretty sight.
I cannot lift a finger
or move a tired toe.
My throat is hot and scratchy,
the answer's simply NO . . .
I cannot go to school today;
I'm awfully sorry too,
this had to happen on the day
my book report was due.

Rebecca Kai Dotlich

Distracted, the Mother Said to Her Boy

Distracted, the mother said to her boy,
"Do you try to upset and perplex and annoy?
Now, give me four reasons—and don't play the fool—
why you shouldn't get up and get ready for school."

Her son replied slowly, "Well, mother, you see,
I can't stand the teachers and they detest me;
and there isn't a boy or a girl in the place
that I like or, in turn, that delights in my face."

"And I'll give you two reasons," she said, "why you ought
get yourself off to school before you get caught;
because, first, you are forty, and, next, you young fool,
it's your job to be there.
You're the head of the school."

Gregory Harrison

Morning Announcements

Good morning, Staff and Students,
take note of what I say.
In school we will have showers
for April starts today.

Some teachers were suspended
for giving too much work.
Today, if you feel lazy,
you'll be allowed to shirk.

We want to find the student
who brought a pig to school.
It is *running* down the hallways,
and that's against the rule.

Today on our lunch menu
are bumblebees in sauce
or chopped cockroach sandwiches
and salad you can toss.

Next year we'll pay our students
for work they do in school . . .
. . . and if you believe these messages,
then you're an APRIL FOOL!

Sylvia Andrews

English Is a Pain! (Pane?)

Rain, reign, rein,
English is a pain.
Although the words
sound just alike,
the spelling's not the same!

Bee, be, B,
I'd rather climb a tree,
than learn to spell
the same old word,
not just one way, but three!

Sight, site, cite,
I try with all my might.
No matter which
I finally choose,
it's not the one that's right!

There, their, they're,
enough to make you swear.
Too many ways
to write one sound,
I just don't think it's fair!

To, two, too,
so what's a kid to do?
I think I'll go
to live on Mars,
and leave this mess with ewe!
(you?)

Shirlee Curlee Bingham

Difficult Math Test

Whoopie! A test! Whoopie! A test!
We're having a difficult test!
We'd also enjoy being kicked by a mule,
then dipped in a caldron of bubbling drool,
but a difficult test is best!

A woodpecker pecking a tune on your head,
then trapped in a mighty collapsible bed,
or dancing barefooted with ol' Frankenstein,
sure, all of these things, why of course, would be fine,
but a difficult test is best!

Or baked in a pie in an oven too hot
and having your fingers all tied in a knot,
then using a chair made of porcupine quills,
can also provide you a great deal of thrills,
but a difficult test is best!

Or put in a vise and then squeezed till you're flat,
or sharing your room with a twenty-foot rat,
and then wearing some tight cactus underwear,
but none of, no none of these things can compare
to the joys of a difficult test!

Robert Scotellaro

How to Eat a Bag Lunch

Banana:
Remove Chiquita
sticker, slap your
friend's back, say, "Ho,
ho, ho," and leave
sticker stuck to shirt.

Cupcake:
Lick off frosting, being
careful to smear it
around mouth and on
chin. Do not eat the
cupcake; crumble it.

Potato Chips:
Leaving out two kids
who are sitting at the
table, give one chip to
kids you like. Prefer to
eat chips with hardly
any brown in them.

Straw:
Shoot off paper, aiming
at the cafeteria
monitor.

Drumstick:
Brag about having fried
chicken. Say that you
had it last night for
dinner. Say that you
have fried chicken at
your house three times
a week, easy.

Announce your favorite part. Wave the drumstick while chanting, "Roast chicken, boo; fried chicken, yay." Pick off skin with fingers; then consume.

Milk:
After spilling, throw carton in garbage can as if it were a basketball. Then move sideways on the bench, shoving the person next to you until the kid at the other end falls off.

Hard-Boiled Egg:
Do not eat, but leave the peeled-off shell and bare egg covered with dirty fingerprints on the cafeteria table.

Paper Bag:
Blow in air, hold closed, and smash. Spend the rest of lunch sitting with the little kids.

Delia Ephron

Happy Hiccup to You

HICCUP! HICCUP!
"Oh no!" I cried. "This can't be true,
what am I supposed to do?"

HICCUP! HICCUP!
"I have to go out on the stage,
when the teacher turns her page."

HICCUP! HICCUP!
"And sing a happy birthday song,
with Fred and Ruth and Matt and John."

HICCUP! HICCUP!
"But I can't sing and hiccup too,
what am I supposed to do?"

HICCUP! HICCUP!
"OH NO! The teacher's turned the page,
now I must go onto the stage."

HICCUP! HICCUP!
"Happy . . . HICCUP . . . to you!
Happy . . . HICCUP . . . to you!
Happy birthday, dear . . . HICCUP!
Happy . . . HICCUP . . . to you!"

("What an awful . . . HICCUP . . . day!")

Kalli Dakos

Public Speaking

Today's the school speech contest.
I feel a little sick.
I hate to talk in front of crowds,
but I've a little trick.

I picture the whole audience
is sitting right out there
without a stitch of clothing on
except their underwear.

It's easy then to read or talk
when all the while I'm peeking.
Just try it if you are like me
and don't like public speaking.

Bill Dodds

The Aliens Have Landed!

The aliens have landed!
It's distressing, but they're here.
They piloted their flying saucer
through our atmosphere.

They landed like a meteor
engulfed in smoke and flame.
Then out they climbed immersed in slime
and burbled as they came.

Their hands are greasy tentacles.
Their heads are weird machines.
Their bodies look like cauliflower
and smell like dead sardines.

Their blood is liquid helium.
Their eyes are made of granite.
Their breath exudes the stench of foods
from some unearthly planet.

And if you want to see these
sickly, unattractive creatures,
you'll find them working in your school;
they all got jobs as teachers!

Kenn Nesbitt

Dinnertime

David asks for his dessert
Peggy wants to press her skirt
she has dance class and she's late
David says he cannot wait
Mike is giving him a ride
he'll just go and wait outside
Father tells him he will not
David mutters thanks a lot
Ann says she expects a call
Benjamin won't eat at all
Mother starts to serve the pie
Benjamin begins to cry
Mother asks him what is wrong
Father says the tea's too strong
Ann gets up to get the phone
Benjamin begins to moan
Peggy says her tights are torn
David says he hears a horn
Father says to finish first
David says that he will burst
Peggy says it isn't fair
Ann has on her other pair
now she will be late for class
Benjamin upsets his glass
David's taking tiny bites
Ann is taking off the tights
David says the crust is tough

Mother says she's had enough
Father says it's not too bad
Mother says she's going mad
David wiggles like a mouse
that is dinner at our house

Mary Ann Hoberman

The Spaghetti Challenge

My mom's spaghetti is the best;
no other mom can beat it;
and every time she cooks it
I can hardly wait to eat it.

I twist the strands around my fork
with wonderful control,
but as I raise them to my mouth
they fall back in the bowl.

I twirl the noodles once again
with all the skill I'm able,
but as I lift them up to eat
they tumble to the table.

I spin my fork; spaghetti winds
around and round once more;
but as it nears my waiting lips
it slithers to the floor.

My mom's spaghetti is the best;
no other mom can beat it;
but I would like it better
if I got a chance to eat it.

Leslie D. Perkins

I Ate a Ton of Sugar

I ate a ton of sugar.
It made me very sweet.
It also made me very round—
now I can't find my feet.

Alice Gilbert

If We Had Lunch at the White House

If we were invited
to the White House for lunch,
Brian wouldn't be able
to steal Lolane's chips.
And Karen couldn't squish up
her milk carton,
after she blew bubbles into her milk,
and Seth couldn't crawl under the table,
chasing his lost pistachio nuts,
and Annie couldn't say
her Spanish rice tasted so yucky,
she would *puke* if she ate it.

Sometimes we think about
eating lunch at the White House,
and all the manners we'd need,
how we'd have to sit very still,
and think before we speak,
and talk in whispers,
and keep our feet on the floor,
and never take a bite—
not even a tasting bite—
until everyone had been served.

Maybe someday
we'll be ready
for lunch at the White House,
but not today,

because at lunch,
Jamal made faces
in his mashed potatoes,
and Patrick sucked Jell-O
up a straw,
and Susan frosted her carrot cake
with ketchup,
and ate it!
And Karen blew so many bubbles
in her milk
that it overflowed
and white, airy foam
covered the table,
and the floor,
and Karen,
and two giant bubbles
landed on our teacher's watch,
and he said,

"I don't think we're ready
for lunch at the White House
. . . . yet!"

Kalli Dakos

53

The Burp

Pardon me for being so rude.
It was not me, it was my food.
It got so lonely down below,
it just popped up to say hello.

Anonymous

Greasy, Grimy Gopher Guts

Great green gobs of greasy, grimy gopher guts,
mutilated monkey meat,
little birdies' dirty feet,
French-fried eyeballs in a sauce of porpoise pus.
And me without a spoon.

Anonymous

Fast Food

Some witches by the roadside
are selling fast-food snacks,
big bubbling warthog pizzas
and dumplings filled with tacks.

They stir things in a caldron
and slap them on a dish,
hot pimple-breaded lizards
and moldy cactus fish,

Some gooey red-eyed fritters
all rolled in spider dough,
some slippery dragon molars,
and boiled fish bones to go.

They're cooking up some freckles
and bats they plucked from caves.
They're using giant caldrons,
they're using microwaves.

They're giving plastic chopsticks,
and you don't have to wait.
They're serving green slime gravy
on worms that palpitate.

And if you're really lucky,
they'll serve you some dessert.
It's something cold and oozy,
on squirming bug-filled dirt.

Robert Scotellaro

Should I?

Would I, could I,
should I try to
eat a slug or
would I die?

Would it slide down
sluggishly or
wiggle, squiggle
buggishly?

Would it stick and
slime my tongue or
glide down swiftly
to my lung?

That might make me
awful dead. Think I'll
eat a worm instead.

Joyce Armor

Bleezer's Ice Cream

I am Ebenezer Bleezer,
I run BLEEZER'S ICE CREAM STORE,
there are flavors in my freezer
you have never seen before,
twenty-eight divine creations
too delicious to resist,
why not do yourself a favor,
try the flavors on my list:

TODAY'S

COCOA MOCHA MACARONI
TAPIOCA SMOKED BALONEY
CHECKERBERRY CHEDDAR CHEW
CHICKEN CHERRY HONEYDEW
TUTTI-FRUTTI STEWED TOMATO
TUNA TACO BAKED POTATO
LOBSTER LITCHI LIMA BEAN
MOZZARELLA MANGOSTEEN
ALMOND HAM MERINGUE SALAMI
YAM ANCHOVY PRUNE PASTRAMI
SASSAFRAS SOUVLAKI HASH
SUKIYAKI SUCCOTASH
BUTTER BRICKLE PEPPER PICKLE
POMEGRANATE PUMPERNICKEL

FLAVORS

PEACH PIMENTO PIZZA PLUM
PEANUT PUMPKIN BUBBLEGUM
BROCCOLI BANANA BLUSTER
CHOCOLATE CHOP SUEY CLUSTER
AVOCADO BRUSSELS SPROUT
PERIWINKLE SAUERKRAUT
COTTON CANDY CARROT CUSTARD
CAULIFLOWER COLA MUSTARD
ONION DUMPLING DOUBLE DIP
TURNIP TRUFFLE TRIPLE FLIP
GARLIC GUMBO GRAVY GUAVA
LENTIL LEMON LIVER LAVA
ORANGE OLIVE BAGEL BEET
WATERMELON WAFFLE WHEAT

I am Ebenezer Bleezer,
I run BLEEZER'S ICE CREAM STORE,
taste a flavor from my freezer,
you will surely ask for more.

Jack Prelutsky

Recipe

First you take a giant bowl
and put a waffle in it,
then you add a bunch of jam
and stir it for a minute.

After that you get a cup
and fill it up with custard,
then dump it in with mushroom soup
and just a little mustard.

Squeeze a lemon right on top,
add peanut butter—oodles,
but don't forget the applesauce
and two big scoops of noodles.

Then nuke it in the microwave.
That's it, you've got a winner.
Get the plates out now and yell,
"Come and get it! Dinner!"

Joyce Armor

Mother Doesn't Want a Dog

Mother doesn't want a dog.
Mother says they smell,
and never sit when you say sit,
or even when you yell.
And when you come home late at night
and there is ice and snow,
you have to go back out because
the dumb dog has to go.

Mother doesn't want a dog.
Mother says they shed,
and always let the strangers in
and bark at friends instead,
and do disgraceful things on rugs,
and track mud on the floor,
and flop upon your bed at night
and snore their doggy snore.

Mother doesn't want a dog.
She's making a mistake.
Because, more than a dog, I think
she will not want this snake.

Judith Viorst

A Very Stubborn Polar Bear

A very stubborn polar bear
got hold of my new underwear.
I warned him that they wouldn't fit.
But did he listen? Not one bit.
He solved the problem well, instead,
by wearing them upon his head.

Linda Knaus

My Dog

My dog is such a gentle soul,
although he's big it's true.
He brings the paper in his mouth.
He brings the postman too.

Max Fatchen

Dumb Dog

I have a dog—
he's real, real dumb,
so when you call,
he will not come.

A stick I toss
he will not catch;
he scratches fleas
when I say "Fetch!"

The *Daily News*
he never brings;
he much prefers
the neighbor's things.

When he smells bad,
we soap him up;
he quickly rolls
in stinky stuff.

He chews my shoes,
then wags his tail;
he should be put
in doggie jail!

Shirlee Curlee Bingham

Dapple Gray

I had a great big elephant,
his name was Dapple Gray.
He was a sweet and gentle pet,
though he got in the way.
He knocked my playhouse over
and squished a chair or two.
He flattened sister's potty—
we followed him with glue.
But what was really scary
was when he took a nap,
for he was only happy
when curled up in my lap.

Robert Scotellaro

Away Down South

Away down south where bananas grow,
a grasshopper stepped on an elephant's toe.
The elephant cried with tears in his eyes,
"Pick on someone your own size."

Anonymous

Little Birdie in the Sky

Little birdie in the sky
dropped some white stuff in my eye.
I'm not angry. I won't cry.
I'm just glad that cows don't fly.

Anonymous

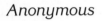

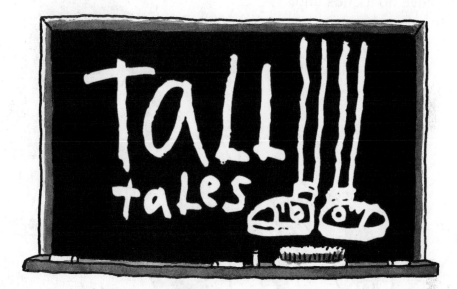

Molly Peters

Little Molly Peters
stuck her finger up her nose.
She pulled it out, examined it,
and wiped it on her clothes.

Now Molly is a lovely girl,
that's really not the issue.
But she will have no friends until
she learns to use a tissue.

Bill Dodds

Little Jimmy Dawson

Now Jimmy Dawson's hearing
was surely most acute.
He'd hear a lint piece falling
from off his father's suit.

He'd hear the flowers growing,
and two cottonballs collide,
the sound of puddles drying—
it kept him occupied.

When listening to a conch shell,
he heard, not just the sea,
but pearls in oysters forming,
as clear as clear could be.

He'd hear a pimple blossom
upon his sister's face—
and hear a new sun rising,
light traveling through space.

But then a strange thing happened—
his mom called him in from play.
Then Jimmy's perfect hearing
completely went away.

Robert Scotellaro

Doing a Good Deed

At the foot of the hill, the ice-cream truck
drove into a mudhole and got stuck.
We helped the driver back on the road.
But first we had to lighten the load.
When we had helped a gallon apiece,
the driver phoned the Chief of Police,
who drove a pole into the sludge
and measured five feet of chocolate fudge
that had to be lightened. Well, we turned to
and helped the man. What else could we do?
I even called my Boy Scout Troop.
By then there was nothing left but soup.
Still, ice-cream soup is very good.
And we wanted to help as much as we could.
It was our good deed for the day
to help the man get on his way.
At last we pulled him out of the muck,
and he drove away in his empty truck,
thanking us all for helping him out.
That made us happy. For there's no doubt
we must help our neighbor as much as we can.
Especially when he's the ice-cream man.

John Ciardi

Tables Turned

The ghost of bold Ned Kelly
came to haunt my Auntie Nellie,
but when it saw her in the light
it was the ghost that got the fright.

Michael Dugan

73

Old Man

There was an old man from Peru
who dreamed he was eating his shoe,
he awoke in the night
in a terrible fright,
and found that his dream was quite true.

Anonymous

Isaac Newton

Sir Isaac Newton sure was smart,
beneath the apple tree.
When one fell off and hit his head,
he said, "Wow, gravity!"

For Newton was a genius
and not a common slouch.
A genius cries "Gravity!"
Most others just say "ouch!"

Calvin Miller

The Chap Who Disappeared

There was a drowsy sort of chap
who went upstairs to take a nap.

At least that's where he thought he went.
But he was living in a tent.

It's true he hadn't pitched it yet,
which may have caused him to forget

He hadn't brought a single stair
to climb up to what wasn't there.

Or it may be he never knew
two-story tents are very few.

So few that there are none at all.
Which left him in the upper hall

Of nowhere. Which may well explain
why he was never seen again.

John Ciardi

Say What?

One fine October morning
in April, last July,
the moon fell on my window,
the rain shone in the sky.
The flowers sang quite sweetly,
the birds were in full bloom,
I dumped the neighbors' garbage
inside our dining room.
My parents always praise me
for sneaking out of school.
They tell me not to study,
so I won't be a fool.
My favorite food is spinach,
it makes my muscles small.
Each day I'm growing shorter,
soon I'll be eight feet tall.
I'm saving up my money,
to throw it all away.
I hope this poem annoys you,
so have a happy day.

Bruce Lansky

The Baby Ate the Dog Food

The baby ate the dog food.
She ate up every bit.
And now she barks when I say *speak*
and stays when I say *sit.*

Her ears are looking furry,
and she's grown a funny tail.
I even heard her growling
at the man who brings the mail.

She scratches fleas and mites, and then
she piddles on the floor.
She chews on shoes and slippers,
and she scratches at the door.

I am not sure whom I should call,
the doctor or the vet.
And how do I tell Mama
that her baby's now the pet?

I'm teaching her to fetch.
She's playing dead and rolling over.
The baby ate the dog food up.
Now what will we feed Rover?

Malia Haberman-Sperry

Popeye the Sailor Man

I'm Popeye, the sailor man.
I live in a moving van.
I go where I'm sent
and I save on the rent,
I'm Popeye, the sailor man.

I'm Popeye, the sailor man.
I live in a caravan.
I open the door
and I fall through the floor,
I'm Popeye, the sailor man.

I'm Popeye, the sailor man.
I live in a garbage can.
It's cramped and it's crude,
but I get lots of food,
I'm Popeye, the sailor man.

I'm Popeye, the sailor man.
I'm doing the best I can.
I eat all my spinach,
I fight to the finish,
I'm Popeye, the sailor man.

Esther L. Nelson

The Insult

(Only read this to someone if: (a) they are much smaller
than you, or: (b) you're an extremely fast runner!)

Look at that horrible thing on your neck!
It's terrible! Look in the mirror and check.
It's spotty and hairy and ugly and red,
but no need to panic. It's only your head!

Colin McNaughton

I Love You Not

I love you I love you,
I love you so well,
if I had a skunk
I would give you a smell.

If I were a dog
I would give you a bite.
If I were a witch
I would give you a fright.

If I were a bathtub
I'd give you a splash.
If I were a fungus
I'd give you a rash.

I love you so much
that I won't tell a lie,
I promise we'll marry
the day that I die.

Bruce Lansky

The Eyes Have It

If you can't see a
thing without a light
If you can't read this
This rhyme exactly
right If you bump
into lamp-posts in
the street Or fail to
recognize the friends
you meet If you trip
over every letter-box
Or go to school
wearing unmatching
socks If you walk
under every
bus that passes
You need
glasses

Susan Stranks

Ned Nott

Ned Nott was shot
and Sam Shott was not.
So it is better to be Shott
than Nott.
Some say Nott
was not shot.
But Shott says
he shot Nott.
Either the shot Shott shot
at Nott
was not shot,
or Nott was shot.
If the shot Shott shot
shot Nott,
then Nott was shot,
but if the shot Shott shot
shot Shott,
then Shott was shot, not Nott.
However, the shot Shott shot
shot not Shott, but Nott.

Anonymous

Betty Botter

Betty Botter
bought some butter.
"But," she said,
"the butter's bitter.
If I put it
in my batter,
it will make
my batter bitter.
But a bit
of better butter—
that would make
my batter better."

So she bought
a bit of butter,
better than
her bitter butter.
And she put it
in her batter,
and the batter
was not bitter.
So 'twas better
Betty Botter
bought a bit
of better butter!

Anonymous

Alphabet Protest

Have you heard that Congress might soon pass a law
that would change Ks to Bs and all Bs to Ks?
I'll tell you, I'm strictly opposed to such laws.
That would change everything that we must write or say.
Why, if all Bs were Ks and all Ks were Bs,
the parrots would sleep in Kanana trees,
and we'd go to the zoo to see Bangaroos,
ZeKras and yaBs with spots on their noses
and Boala Kears and wild Kuffaloes.

If this Kill is passed, our Krains will be corB,
the Statue of LiKerty will be in New YorB.
You'd better liBe eating your meals with a forB
and sandwiches made out of KarKeque porB.
Concerning vacations, I'll only say yucB!
Would you go to Disney to see Donald DucB
or Minnie or MicBie Mouse? What rotten LucB!

This Kill would have mommies Biss KaKies goodnight
or rocB them in rocBing chairs till it was light.
Koys would sleep in KunB Keds in their Kedroom.
And Kig KlacB convertiKles sure would have headroom.
Do you see now why Congress must not pass this Kill?
ThinB of the poor souls who live in MilwauBee,
AlKuquerque or Bansas or those in BentucBee.
You must write to Congress on Capitol Hill
and say, "Leave our letters alone, if you will.
All Ks must be Ks and Bs must be Bs.

We voters demand that you listen up, please . . .
No federal tamp'ring with our ABCs!"

Calvin Miller

88

I Thought a Thought

I thought a thought.
But the thought I thought wasn't the thought I thought I thought.
If the thought I thought I thought had been the thought
I thought,
I wouldn't have thought so much.

Anonymous

Mary Had a Little Ham

Mary had a little ham
with scrambled eggs and toast with jam.
Then she had a little cake,
and then she had a bellyache.

Bruce Lansky

Mary Had Some Bubble Gum

Mary had some bubble gum,
she chewed it long and slow,
and everywhere that Mary went
her gum was sure to go.
She chewed the gum in school one day,
which was against the rule,
the teacher took her pack away
and chewed it after school.

Anonymous

Mary Had a Little Lamb

Mary had a little lamb,
a lobster, and some prunes,
a glass of milk, a piece of pie,
and then some macaroons.

It made the busy waiters grin
to see her order so,
and when they carried Mary out,
her face was white as snow.

Anonymous

94

There Was an Old Woman

There was an old woman
who lived in a shoe;
with so many children
what else could she do?

Their home had no windows,
no doors, and no locks—
the kids were all happy
but smelled like old socks.

Bill Dodds

Yankee Doodle's Monkey Ride

Yankee Doodle went to town,
riding on a monkey.
He had to take a shower quick
because he smelled so funky.

Bruce Lansky

Mrs. Doodle

Mrs. Doodle went to town,
riding on a gator.
She didn't feed the gator,
so the hungry gator ate 'er.

Bruce Lansky

Hickory, Dickory, Dock!

Hickory, dickory, dock!
A goat just ate my sock.
Then took my shirt
for his dessert.
Hickory, dickory, dock!

Robert Scotellaro

Row, Row, Row Your Boat

Row, row, row your boat,
gently down the stream,
until you hit the waterfall—
then you'll start to scream.

Bill Dodds

Toothpaste

There is toothpaste on my fingers.
There is toothpaste in my nose.
There is toothpaste on the mirror
in a hundred squiggly rows.

There is toothpaste on my pj's,
how it got there you can guess.
There are gobs of gooey toothpaste
in the toilet, what a mess.

There is toothpaste in the bathtub,
overflowing on the floor.
It's congealing on the ceiling
and it's dripping down the door.

Every time I squeeze the toothpaste,
it sprays north and west and south.
There is toothpaste almost everywhere,
except inside my mouth!

Stan Lee Werlin

Bathtub Rules

Don't go standing on your head.
From somersaults refrain.
Be careful not to let your nose
get stuck down in the drain.
Don't bump your elbow on the tiles.
Don't stump your little toe.
Don't squirt shampoo into your eyes
or bathe with buffalo.
Don't drink up any water.
Don't eat up any soap,
or you'll be on the chilly end
of a doctor's stethoscope!

Eileen Spinelli

I Saw You

I saw you in the ocean,
I saw you in the sea,
I saw you in the bathtub.
Oops! Pardon me.

Anonymous

How to Delay Your Bedtime

Refuse to turn off the TV.
Say, "All my friends watch this show."

Say, "No fair!" when you're told to go to bed.
Then ask, "Why can't I stay up till ten
like all my friends?"

When Dad says, "If all your friends
jumped off the Brooklyn Bridge,
would you jump too?"
sneer, "Yes!"

Whine, "I'm too tired to walk upstairs to bed."
Make Dad carry you up the stairs.

Pout, "I'm too tired to brush my teeth."
Wait till Dad squeezes the toothpaste
onto your brush and starts brushing
your teeth for you.
Then groan, "Ouch, you're hurting me."

When Mom comes in to say good night
and asks you to pick up your clothes,
yawn, "I'm too tired to pick up my clothes."
Watch while Mom picks them up for you.

Beg, "I need a bedtime story."
When Mom finishes the story,
ask, "And then what happened?"

Tell her, "That story got me excited.
Now I need a backrub to make me sleepy."
When Mom starts rubbing, give directions:
"Rub a little higher.
No, a little to the left.

No, more in the middle."
When Mom stops rubbing,
grumble, "I was just starting to feel sleepy—
don't stop now."

When Mom says, "For the last time, good night!"
whine, "I'm thirsty.
Can I have a glass of water?"
When Mom asks you to promise
you won't wet the bed,
say, "I promise"—but cross your fingers.

Start crying.
When Dad comes to comfort you,
sob, "There's a monster under my bed."
When he turns on the lights,
you'll see it's only your shoes, socks, crayons,
and the toy you got last Christmas,
but only played with once because you lost it.
Tell him, "Leave the door open
so I can see the hall light!"
When he opens up the door
plead, "Open it wider!"

When Dad leaves,
get the toy from under your bed
and play with it in the light
shining through your doorway.

Bruce Lansky

Knight Warning

This is what his mother said
when little Knight went up to bed:

"Get up in the night, My Dear, you must!
Don't wet the bed, or you might rust!"

Babs Bell Hajdusiewicz

CREDITS

TITLE INDEX

AUTHOR INDEX

What People Say about Bruce Lansky's Poetry:

What librarians say:

"Bruce Lansky's poetry books are so funny, we can't keep them on our library shelves." —Lynette Townsend, Lomarena Elementary, Laguna Hills, California

"As soon as the library opens in the morning, there is a line of children waiting for Bruce Lansky's poetry books." —Kay Winek, Pattison Elementary, Superior, Wisconsin

What teachers say:

"Some of my students don't like reading, but once they open one of Lansky's poetry books, I can't get them to close it." —Suzanna Thompson, Holy Name Elementary, Wayzata, MN

"Bruce Lansky turns reluctant readers into avid readers."—Sharon Klein, Clardy Elementary, Kansas City, MO

"Bruce Lansky is the 'Pied Piper of Poetry.' He gets children excited about reading and writing poetry."—Mary Wong, Explorer Middle School, Phoenix, AZ

"There's no doubt about it—Bruce Lansky is the king of giggle poetry."—Jody Bolla, North Miami Elementary, Aventura, FL

What critics say:

"Guaranteed to elicit laughs when read alone or aloud to a class."—*Booklist*

"When I read any of his poems, it's giggles galore."—*Instructor* magazine

What kids say about Bruce Lansky's gigglepoetry.com:

"I really like your site. I used to hate poetry, but you guys make it fun."—Christina, Texas

"Even though I'm from outer space, I can speak and read your language. These poems are cool. On my planet, all we ever do is sit around and watch TV." —Me, Outer Space

"I really love this website. It is awesome! It gives me stuff to do when I am grounded." —Tiffany, Enid, Oklahoma

"I think these poems are the best poems ever!!! If you ever get down, they will make you feel better!!! —Hadassah, Augusta, Georgia

"My teacher wanted to read some poems. I gave her some I found on gigglepoetry.com. The whole class laughed like mad zombies." —Jolin, Singapore

Poetry Books by Bruce Lansky:

Kids Pick the Funniest Poems
Miles of Smiles
If Pigs Could Fly
Poetry Party

Happy Birthday to Me!
The New Adventures of Mother Goose
No More Homework! No More Tests!
Sweet Dreams

For information about inviting poet/author Bruce Lansky to your school or conference, or to order a free Meadowbrook Press catalog, write or call toll-free:

Meadowbrook Press, 5451 Smetana Drive, Minnetonka, MN 55343, 800-338-2232
www.meadowbrookpress.com   www.gigglepoetry.com